IMAGES OF E

Barnwood, Hucclecote
and Brockworth

An aerial view of Brockworth, probably c.1927, looking across to Robinswood Hill and the Severn valley. Note the open space now covered by housing development. The airfield was all grass at this stage, the hard-surfaced runways were in place at the beginning of the Second World War.

IMAGES OF ENGLAND

Barnwood, Hucclecote and Brockworth

Alan Sutton

NONSUCH

An almost vertical view of Hucclecote, 1937. The main road goes from the left (near Carisbrooke Road) to the right (near Barnwood Garage). Note the medieval ridge and furrow clearly visible in the fields.

First published 1994
This new pocket edition 2005
Text and images unchanged from first edition

Nonsuch Publishing Limited
The Mill, Brimscombe Port,
Stroud, Gloucestershire, GL5 2QG
www.nonsuch-publishing.com

British Library Cataloguing in Publication Data.
A catalogue record for this book is available from the British Library.

ISBN 1-84588-100-1

Typesetting and origination by Nonsuch Publishing Limited.
Printed in Great Britain by Oaklands Book Services Limited.

Contents

A detail of the crowd scene from the photograph on page 102. The visit of Sydney Pickles, the intrepid aeronaut created great local interest over the Easter weekend of 1913.

Introduction

Barnwood, Hucclecote and Brockworth have served as dormitory settlements to Gloucester for at least 2,000 years. Within a few years of the Roman invasion of AD 43, Cirencester became the second largest town, and Gloucester one of the four colonia in the Roman province of Britannia. Between these two important towns a road was built, and this road, Ermin Street, served as the line of communication along which the parishes illustrated in this book developed. Roman remains at Hucclecote include two villas, and the large villa at Great Witcombe, just east of Brockworth, further demonstrates the dormitory importance of this area, the result of access afforded by the Ermin Street route. The road has remained in constant use for 1,900 years and was the main route eastwards to London.

All three parishes are mentioned in Domesday Book and were almost certainly continuously occupied settlements from the Roman era, right through the Dark Ages, to the Norman Conquest of 1066. The Domesday survey records that Barnwood was part of the holdings of St Peter's Abbey but, unfortunately, does not list the number of villagers and smallholders separately. Archbishop Stigand held Hucclecote and the male population consisted 11 villagers and 5 smallholders, with 11 ploughs. There was a mill, and woodland one league long by half a league wide. Hugh Donkey held Brockworth from the king. The population was 8 villagers, 6 smallholders, a priest, 2 free men and a reeve; between them they had 15 ploughs. In addition there were 4 slaves, a mill and woodland one league long by half a league wide.

The Domesday survey was on the basis of heads of family and did not include wives and children, so the true population was obviously greater. The population of Hucclecote, including families, would have been in the region of sixty to eighty. By the time of Samuel Rudder's history of the county, published in 1779, nearly seven hundred years later, the populations had grown quite significantly. Barnwood had 180 inhabitants in forty houses. Hucclecote is included with Churchdown, as at that time it was not a parish but a tithing of Churchdown, and the Churchdown parish had 131 households and a population of 630. It is reasonable to suppose that Hucclecote was between a third and a half of that total. Brockworth had fifty houses and a population of 253.

Between Domesday and Rudder, there are a number of surveys. One of particular interest is the military survey of the county taken in 1608 to assess the male population between the ages of sixteen and sixty suitable for military service. In this survey, Barnwood and Wotton (together) could supply 65 men, Hucclecote could supply 29, and Brockworth 43. Most of the Hucclecote men were 'husbandmen', with the occasional labourer, smith or cordwainer. In Brockworth there was a distinct difference. There was a considerable contingent of husbandmen, but also a large number of labourers and other artisans, including smiths, tailors and carpenters.

A rural summer scene looking towards Cooper's Hill, *c.*1930.

The history of the three parishes is not unusual but does contain strands of significant interest. Lying closest to the city, Barnwood has the structure and history of an outer suburb. Fortunately it missed suburbanization in the nineteenth century and, with its attractive Norman church, retained a considerable rural charm beyond the railway line. Hucclecote, being part of Churchdown parish, lacked the typical village organization around a parish church. As a tithing of Churchdown, however, it stood as a separate community, and lay stretched out along the Ermin Street line. Until 1851 it shared the parish church on Churchdown Hill but in that year the Victorian Gothic church was built to serve the rising population. Brockworth alone enjoyed the form and structure of an English village. Alongside the late Norman and thirteenth-century church stands Brockworth Court, a sixteenth- to eighteenth-century house built originally for the last prior of Llanthony. But even this village cannot be said to be typical. The church and court did not provide the centre of the village, and the Ermin Street line of communication had much influence on the usual nucleated village form which would have had the church as the centre. The village was haphazardly laid out, with Ermin Street a popular attraction for settlement.

In between Hucclecote and Brockworth lies another historic site. This site goes into the history books for an event that occurred in the twentieth century, not the first century of the Roman engineers' road layouts. It was on 8 April 1941, amidst considerable secrecy, that the world's first jet aircraft first left the ground – in short hops of 100 and 200 yards – when P.E.G. Sayers, the GAC chief test pilot undertook taxiing tests on the Hucclecote airfield for the Whittle jet prototype.

The Gloster Aircraft Company had a tremendous impact on Hucclecote and Brockworth. The airfield came into being in 1915 as the Air Board aircraft acceptance park, a War Office department that had the responsibility for checking and commissioning aeroplanes built for the government. The Air Manufacturing Company had a factory

A view of the maypole on Cooper's Hill c.1939, looking down towards Hucclecote and Brockworth with some of the G.A.C. works.

in Cheltenham for building aircraft, and the Hucclecote-Brockworth site was ideal for receiving the machines on completion. They were delivered by road on Ford lorries.

In 1917 a new company was formed, 50 per cent of which was owned by the Air Manufacturing Company, the other 50 per cent by A.W. Martyn and George Holt Thomas. Thus was born the Gloucestershire Aircraft Company Limited. Their manufacturing was still at the H.H. Martyn factory in Cheltenham, but by 1921 they had started renting some of the hangars at Hucclecote from the Air Board. In 1926 the company simplified its name, changing it to 'Gloster', and in 1928 they bought all of the 200 acre site and office accommodation for £15,000 and moved all operations to Hucclecote.

The company was taken over in 1934 by Hawker Aircraft Limited, and from that time on Hawker designs were also built at the site. In 1938, as part of the great national expansion programme, Gloster Aircraft was instructed to build a new large factory, and by the end of 1940 the 'shadow' factory was built at Brockworth with a manufacturing floor area of 24 acres. At the same time a hard-surfaced runway was built to replace the grass strip which had restricted activity in wet weather.

The Company built 2,750 Hawker Hurricanes in four batches between 1940 and 1942. This was followed by the Hurricane's successor – the Hawker Typhoon. The production of Typhoons ended in 1945, by which time a total of 3,330 had been built. The production of Typhoons is illustrated on pages 111 and 112.

The pioneer work by Frank Whittle led to the development of the E28/39, usually known as the 'Whittle Jet'. This first left the ground at Hucclecote on 8 April 1941, and a week later full-scale flight tests were carried out at Cranwell in Lincolnshire, where the less-populated surrounding area was more conducive to the maintenance of secrecy than were the built-up areas around Gloucester and Cheltenham. Before the first flight of this prototype jet, the Air Ministry had given the go-ahead for a production jet fighter and a specification had been issued. This was followed in August 1941 with an order for 300 jet fighters, and the name of 'Meteor' was chosen by the Air Ministry, against the wishes of Gloster Aircraft, who preferred 'Annihilator', 'Ace' or 'Reaper'.

The first flight took place on 12 January 1944. The Meteor entered operational service several months later and was used initially against the V1 attacks on London. They were sent across the channel in 1945 but were not allowed to fly over enemy-occupied territory as a precaution against their falling into hostile hands, and they never engaged Luftwaffe jet fighters in combat.

By the end of the war GAC were employing 14,000 people in forty locations in Gloucestershire, but the majority were employed at the Hucclecote and Brockworth sites. After the war the production of Meteors continued until 1954. It was followed by the Javelin, which entered service with the RAF in 1956. By 1960 Gloster Aircraft had produced over 4,000 jet aeroplanes in a nineteen year period. However, cancellation by the Government of the Gloster F153D and the changes in the Defence White Paper of 1957 proved to be the death knell for the company, and the Hawker Siddeley Company decided to close the Gloucester manufacturing plant for aircraft. By 1959 most manufacturing on the site, including that of parts for the Vulcan bomber and the Blue Steel rocket, had been on a sub-contracting basis to other companies. In that year the company started diversification into vending machine and road tanker and trailer manufacture.

In 1963 the Gloster name disappeared when Hawker Siddeley Aviation became the regrouped Hawker Aircraft Manufacturing Company. A new company was formed to take over the vending machine and road vehicle manufacture, and the name of Gloster Saro Limited was registered and business transferred. On 6 April 1964 the site was sold to Gloucester Trading Estates and an important era in the history of Gloucester and of British aviation came to an end.

The development of Barnwood, Hucclecote and Brockworth along the linear route created by the Romans was greatly boosted by the arrival of the aircraft industry. But the development would probably have happened anyway, even if at a slightly later date, because of the natural growth of the city of Gloucester. The photographs in this book record some early views from the nineteenth century, but most are from the period between 1900 and 1950 and they show how the first half of this century has been formative in creating the structure of the three parishes as they appear to us today. A few photographs record the further structural changes to the shape of the parishes by the building of the Barnwood bypass and the M5.

The views here record a community in change, an evolution from a village life, including farms, to a suburban community. They provide a vital record of this metamorphosis for the generations to come.

Unfortunately the parishes of Barnwood and Brockworth have not received as lavish a treatment in the number of views published as Hucclecote. This will hopefully be rectified in a future publication and I would welcome hearing from anyone holding photographs of any of the three parishes, especially Barnwood and Brockworth, so that this imbalance can be rectified.

Alan Sutton
February 1994

One

Barnwood

A view towards Barnwood near the old city boundary, c.1906. Note the electric lamps on the city side, but gas lamps beyond.

A view up hill towards Wotton from the old city boundary, c.1925. This part of the road has never been widened, yet all the houses on the right disappeared long ago.

From previous page: an enlargement from top photograph.

Barnwood Road, 1936. The view is to the east from near Armscroft Road. Work on the replacement bridge can be seen in the distance.

Barnwood Road. A photograph taken from Armscroft Road looking towards the city during the roadworks of 1936.

Barnwood Bridge, a view looking towards Wotton *c.*1920, with the raised footpath on the left. Evidently illustrating a file of shire horses, but the occasion is unknown. They may have been from a brewery dray.

Barnwood Bridge at an early stage in the works of June 1936. The old span is still in position. This view looking towards Hucclecote.

14

Barnwood Bridge works in the summer of 1936. This view looking towards the city with the new steel span now in position.

Barnwood Bridge, a view from the site of the present roundabout looking towards the city at later stages in the 1936 works.

This montage is of four photographs joined together, showing a panoramic view stretching from Eastern Avenue to the area now covered by the main entrance to Wall's Ice Cream *c.* 1958.

The two bottom photographs, (this page and page 17) are enlargements of the central two pictures from the montage above.

The two pairs of houses on the right were later demolished to make way for the dual carriageway, c.1964.

Barnwood Road, looking west to Barnwood Bridge and Wotton c.1950.

Eastern Avenue, looking south-west from somewhere near the Barnwood Road junction, c.1950. Note the tree-lined rural aspect.

The main road looking to the east from Barnwood roundabout, *c.*1938.

The main road looking east from Barnwood roundabout *c.*1950.

The main road at Barnwood c.1950. W.J. Lyddiatt's garage and post office stores on the left.

The main road at Barnwood with a tram standing at the halt near where the roundabout now is. The building at the left belongs to Wheeler's Nursery, and Barnwood Bridge is just off the picture to the left. This photograph c.1930.

Barnwood Road, looking towards Barnwood Bridge c.1938.

Barnwood Road to the east near the Limes, *c*.1938.

The main road at Barnwood at the junction with Grove Crescent, and showing part of Barnwood School, *c*.1938.

Barnwood Road, viewpoint east of the school, c.1938.

Barnwood Road to the north-west. This photograph is taken from opposite the Moors, the fence of which can be seen on the extreme right of the picture, c.1938.

Barnwood Road to the north-west, nearer the school, *c*.1938.

Barnwood Avenue *c*.1950 with Robinswood Hill in the distance.

A view straight along Barnwood Avenue *c.*1900. It seems likely that this is looking northwards to the main road, the bridge over the brook is to the foreground.

Barnwood Avenue at the entrance to the main road in 1938. The gate pillars provided the grand entrance to the drive of a large private house.

The main road through Barnwood, a view to the east from near Barnwood Avenue, c.1955.

A view along Barnwood Avenue c.1950. Note the gas standard lamps. These were being installed on housing developments up until the end of the 1930s. This seems to contrast strangely with the fact that the city had had electric street lighting, replacing gas, for almost thirty years by the time of these installations.

Another view of Barnwood Avenue, presumably taken at the same time as the picture above, and that on page 25. Barnwood Court would be just off the right of this picture.

The main road through Barnwood, looking towards Wotton, c.1906. The long boarded fence and wall of 'The Moors' on the right will be remembered by many. Note the succession of 'stop' signs on standards, showing that in those days trams could be stopped at very frequent intervals.

Barnwood Road with 'The Moors' on the right, c.1930.

Barnwood Road, a view to the north-west showing the corner of Coney Hill Road on the left, c.1950.

A similar view to that above, but taken from further back and dated approximately five years later.

The sluice on Coney Hill Road discharging the water from the lakes into the brook. The road was then called Barnwood Church Lane. This photograph c.1950.

Barnwood Church Lane, c.1950. The wall of Barnwood House grounds is on the right with the sluice as shown on page 31.

The main road looking east, from near Coney Hill Road (Barnwood Church Lane), c.1938. The wall on the right was to the the Barnwood House mental hospital. Part of the old mansion still remains today.

The main road looking towards Barnwood with the tram lines visible in the road. The large house is Barnwood Lodge, with Upton Lane just behind it. This photograph *c*.1926.

An aerial view from the Oxstalls area on the Cheltenham Road, looking across Elmbridge Road, Wall's factory, Barnwood and Hucclecote, 1969.

Two

Hucclecote
Along the Main Road

A pair of thatched cottages on the main road at the corner of Chosen Way. The old gentleman is understood to be Richard Colwell, the local Methodist pioneer and this photograph may be at about 1900 when he was ninety years old.

The same thatched cottages on the main road at the corner of Chosen Way. The cottage on the right is where some of the Methodist meetings were held until the church was built in 1848. This view c.1938.

From previous page: a detail from the picture on page 41.

Woodbine and Streatham with Hucclecote Cottage, these are now 23, 25 and 27 Hucclecote Road, between the garage and Chosen Way. This photograph c.1965.

Chosen Way corner, the 'Grey House' built c.1857 and the butcher's shop dating from about 1920. This photograph c.1957. This area is now covered by the telecommunications building.

Mr G. Gwilliam with his milk float, in front of his house on the main road at the corner of Dinglewell, on the site now covered by the chemist's shop. This house was a victim of the enemy bomb which fell just opposite in 1942. This view *c*.1905.

Right: A house near the Royal Oak. From *c*.1920 this was the 'police station'. This view *c*.1932. Demolished soon after 1970.

Opposite above: A small shop near Chosen Way, *c*.1957. For much of the last century and well into this century this building, small as it is, was occupied as two separate dwellings.

Opposite below: Towards the main road from a point just inside Dinglewell. The new building on the left was the fish shop, built on the site of houses destroyed by an enemy bomb. This view *c*.1970, since when this, and other buildings towards the Royal Oak have been cleared away.

The Royal Oak, *c*.1908.

The Royal Oak, *c*.1930. The pub was demolished in 1957, and the business transferred to the house next door which was enlarged for the purpose. The site of the old building is now used as the car park.

Brown's bakery and grocery on the main road, nearly opposite Hillview Road, c.1911. Various businesses have gone on here up to recent times. Now Mr Fox's barbers shop.

The main road, looking east from near Hillview Road, 1939.

A view along main road to the east with Yew Tree House on the left. Next to it, behind the tram standard, is the shoeing forge. The entrance to Yew Tree Farm is to the right-hand bottom corner of this postcard, which probably dates from *c*.1905.

Opposite above: The Methodist Church, opposite Hillview Road, built in 1848 and demolished in 1929 when the new church was built in Carisbrooke Road. The Methodist Church schoolroom is still in use today.

Opposite below: East elevation of Chapel House on the main road between the Methodist graveyard and Yew Tree Farm, probably *c*.1960 when derelict.

Yew Tree House, c.1911.

Yew Tree House, c.1925. Note the brass plate on the fence indicating the doctor's surgery.

Side view of Yew Tree House, with members of the Long Family who lived here for many years. This view believed to be *c.*1880.

Yew Tree House during demolition in 1958.

Elton House, demolished *c.*1906. Elton Villas were built on the site, immediately west of the former vicarage. This is where houses numbered 84 and 86 now stand.

The building on the main road known to older residents as the Vicarage, being the parish vicar's residence from *c.*1852 to *c.*1952. Now divided as numbers 88 and 90. This view *c.*1910.

The Cedars, formerly Cedar Lawn, a photograph from the early years of this century. A block of flats is now on this site.

The Cedars in the course of demolition, 1968. The fine cedar tree was also destroyed.

The main road, looking towards Barnwood, with Larkhay Road on the right, c.1922.

An interesting view of the main road and the original Waggon and Horses Inn, probably dating from the 1870s. Beyond the inn is a house which stood on the subsequent forecourt, almost in front of the stable block, and which had disappeared by 1880.

The old Waggon and Horses Inn, *c.*1900, just prior to demolition, after which the present building was erected on the same site.

The main road, looking east, with part of the new Waggon and Horses Inn, c.1930.

The main road, near the Waggon and Horses Inn, looking east, 1958.

The main road, near the Waggon and Horses Inn, looking west, 1958.

West frontage of the present Waggon and Horses Inn c.1911. adjacent to the bowling green.

The Waggon and Horses Inn, c.1922. Note that the Waggon has now lost its 'Horses'. Perhaps this is the precursor to its losing its name altogether in readiness for it being given some inane new name like 'The Hucc Inn' or 'The Tippler's Haven'.

The Waggon and Horses Inn c.1948 with a fine growth of Viginia Creeper brightening the rather austere dark brick frontage.

Manor House, originally a farmhouse, but for much of the twentieth century divided into two dwellings. The small shop attached from c.1936. The property was demolished in 1967, this photograph dates from 1958. The site is now covered by Glenville Parade, the row of shops opposite the Waggon and Horses, the inn sign of which can be seen on the extreme right of the picture.

Chosen Cottage, photographed early this century.

Penryn and Firgrove on the main road, with the old garage to the right and opposite the new garage premises. This photograph c.1965.

Old Farm Cottage, a good view from a photograph dated 1902. These properties are now 101 and 103 Hucclecote Road.

The tithe barn, which stood almost opposite Hucclecote House, demolished *c*.1935. This site now occupied by houses called Coxmore Close.

Hucclecote House, an early nineteenth-century gentleman's residence, demolished in 1979. The site can be identified by the house on the right-hand edge, still standing, numbered 113 Hucclecote Road.

A horse and milk cart outside the Palmers, probably c.1905.

The Palmers, which stood a few yards west of the Churchdown Lane corner; destroyed by fire in 1911. Part of the thatched barn can be seen to the left of the picture.

Foley House, possibly a corruption of 'the folly', a building of curious composition, often vacant for long periods of time. It was converted into flats c.1945 and demolished in 1971. The end of Green Lane shown on the left-hand side of the photograph.

A woolly gathering in the main road by the tram terminus c.1906. The Palmers on the right, together with the thatched barn that was burnt down in 1928.

The main road, westwards from the bus terminus, photographed in 1939.

'Palmers Cottage', (or 'Top Shop') with Palmers to the left of it. This photograph probably dates to the 1880s and has unfortunately been damaged. Note how Palmers Cottage was definitely divided into two dwellings.

'Top Shop' at about 1913, with a good view of a tram and 'respectable' ladies with parasols.

Palmers Cottage c.1900. Shortly after this a shop was incorporated in the building and later became known as 'The Top Shop'. It was demolished in 1960.

An interesting enlargement of the picture at the bottom of the facing page. The 'Top Shop' was obviously setting itself up as a refreshment house for the sustenance of cyclists; by now cycling was becoming a popular hobby for the middle classes.

Opposite above: Hucclecote terminus. The tram takes up most of the picture, but the corner of Carisbrooke Road is just visible behind the conductor. Note the sign announcing that the Methodist church is to be built here. This dates the picture to *c.*1928.

Opposite below: The 'Top Shop', known as Palmers Cottage, with the Palmers behind *c.*1911, very shortly before Palmers was destroyed by fire.

Above and below: 'The Top Shop' in 1939. This photograph can be accurately dated by the news placards announcing the imminence of war. This is presumably March 1939 when Lord Halifax, the foreign secretary, made some strident speeches in the House of Lords following Hitler's annexation of the remainder of Czechoslovakia.

Above: The main road, westwards from the bus terminus, *c.*1950. The 'Top Shop' on the right was demolished in 1960.

Below: Hucclecote Terminus and 'Top Shop' at about 1911. Note the number of bicycles. During the First World War the tram lines were extended to the Air Board acceptance airfield. See the top picture on page 64.

View from Tram Terminus, Hucclecote, Glos.

The main road, looking towards Brockworth, with Carisbrooke Road on the right. The view is believed to date from 1922. The tramway can be seen continuing towards Brockworth as between 1917 and 1924 it was extended as a wartime measure to serve the aircraft factory.

The main road looking towards Brockworth with Carisbrooke Road on the right-hand side. This photograph dates from 1969, just before the building of the motorway bridge carrying the M5 across the road.

Mrs Colwell and infant standing outside what are now numbers 148 and 150 Hucclecote Road, immediately east of Belmont Avenue.

Beechwood, on the north side of the main road, on the site now occupied by the filling station, c.1939.

An aerial view of Barnwood and Hucclecote from 1984, with the M5 in the foreground.

Opposite: Churchdown Lane, *c.*1904. This was evidently considered picturesque by commercial photographers. The trees were all cut down *c.*1940. This part of the lane has now disappeared.

Three

Hucclecote
off the Main Road

Green Lane, from the war memorial at the main road, *c.*1939.

Parsonage Cottage, Green Lane. The date is unknown, but it still retains its stone roof. Probably *c.*1900.

Green Lane, from near the main road with Parsonage Cottage on the right, c.1950.

Looking towards the main road from the Billbrook Road junction on Green Lane, c.1930.

Green Lane looking towards the main road from a point near the bridge over the brook, 1939.

An enlargement of the picture above with plenty of human interest.

The Croft, now number 43 Green Lane, c.1925.

The Willows, built on the site of an older house which was pulled down c.1916. This house, on the green, still stands but has been enlarged and altered.

Another view of the Willows at the north-west end of the Green, c.1925. Note the neat white wicket fence and gate.

Billbrook Road looking from the Carisbrooke Road direction. The barrier was moved to this position from further along, originally near where the lamp standard appears in the picture. A view from the bad winter of 1963.

Potholes and puddles in Carisbrooke Road, 1959. A view looking towards Churchdown Lane with a glimpse of the 'Top Shop' only a few months prior to demolition.

A summer view along Carisbrooke Road towards the terminus and 'Top Shop', c.1932.

Left: Carisbrooke Road, 1959, at the commencement of the housing development.

Opposite below: Cottage block, Dinglewell, demolished c.1968. New houses, 1 and 3 Dinglewell now stand on this site.

Above: Springbank and Ferndale, Dinglewell. These houses, near the main road, were not built as one unit, and when the German bomb fell in 1942 they came apart and had to be demolished.

Dinglewell, just short of the bridge over the brook, looking along Foxall Road, *c.*1935.

Opposite above: Dinglewell, a snow scene from *c.*1958, towards the main road with junction of Foxall Road just off left bottom corner. Foxall Road is what is now incorrectly called Brookfield Road.

Opposite below: Dinglewell, 1938. Over the bridge and along Foxall Road before roadworks and the rebuilding of the bridge.

Dinglewell extension to join Kingscroft Road, from the former end of Dinglewell, 1939. The open space in the lower left corner is where a large emergency water supply tank stood during the war.

Hill View, number 3 Chosen Way, c.1910. The home of John Long, who was one of the victims of the 1942 German bomb.

Chosen Way, north end, showing the road not yet made up and still a dead end. English's gardens are behind the wall on the right, just before all of this land was taken for housing, c.1959.

Hillview Road from the main road, showing the condition of the carriageway prior to surfacing, c.1934.

Hillview Road after surfacing, 1936.

Larkhay Road, looking away from the main road. A bus stands by the church, probably a special service waiting for children from the school. Cows are making their leisurely way from fields which still existed beyond the school, probably for milking at Yew Tree Farm, 1939.

Hucclecote Church from Larkhay Road. The small original school is in the background with what seems to be a bell turret. This dates the photograph to before 1900 when a larger school was built beyond.

Hucclecote Church at about 1906 from the field opposite with two schools on the left. Note that the church has not yet been extended on that side.

Pitt Mill from the field on the opposite side of Larkhay Road, *c.*1910.

Pitt Mill yard, with a flock of sheep gathered ready for dipping, *c.*1906.

Right: Pitt Mill house, seen along Larkhay Road from the west. A 1970 view to the south-west from the lane, near the mill building.

Below: A 1968 view of Pitt Mill house from the yard, with the house in a state of dereliction.

Pitt Mill c.1962. This appears to be a view 'upstream' along the bed of the now vanished mill race.

The rear of the Pitt Mill house, and side of the old mill building c.1970.

Zoons Court, a winter scene c.1912.

Zoons Court, the farmhouse for some 250 acres of land. This photograph taken c.1965 prior to the building becoming derelict.

St. Bartholomew's Church on the hill top, c.1900. This picture clearly shows the boundary of the old churchyard, with the cottage being on the outside of the churchyard wall.

St. Bartholomew's Church, c.1905.

Yew Tree Cottage, once the Chosen Hill Tea Gardens, near the reservoir on the summit of Churchdown Hill, c.1960.

The rear of Yew Tree Cottage, the 'Chosen Hill Tea Gardens', c.1905.

The occupiers of Yew Tree Cottage at the top of Churchdown Hill did a thriving trade at their 'Chosen Hill Tea Gardens' for the many people who would think nothing of climbing the hill from both Churchdown and Hucclecote. The furniture at this date (c.1905) is rude, but it was a delightful site.

One of the houses at Buscombe Noke, or Oystershell, which evidently also served as a tea garden. This is presumed to be at the rear, c.1903.

A useful panoramic view in times before aerial photographs from aircraft. The line of the main road through Hucclecote and Brockworth can be traced across the centre, and there are very few houses on it; and, of course, there are no aerodrome buildings. To get bearings, it may be mentioned that Millbridge is just off the middle of the right edge. The date of this view must be c.1904.

An agricultural idyll. A view of Churchdown Hill from Churchdown Lane c.1955.

Churchdown Lane, up the incline from Millbridge showing a fine avenue of mature elm trees, c.1906.

Churchdown Lane, looking towards main road, with the house 'Hucclecote Knoll' on the right and a raised path on the left. The junction of the present Zoons Road would be at the extreme right, c.1905.

Churchdown Lane near the bridge over the brook, with Noke in the distance and old Millbridge pump in the foreground, c.1959.

Churchdown Lane, looking south-west with the bus terminus in the distance, *c*.1950.

Churchdown Lane, looking towards Millbridge, *c*.1910. Hucclecote Knoll is on the left, although the house was at that time called 'Oldbury'.

Four

Hucclecote
People & Events

The choir at the main door of the church, possibly on the occasion of the completion of the new organ in 1904. Back row, from left to right: Mr H. Piff, Miss Corbett, Miss G. Murray-Browne, Miss Wood, Mrs Hannam-Clarke, Miss Hannam-Clarke, Mrs Gill, Miss B. Murray-Browne, Miss Corbett, Mr G. Long and Mr R. Page. Middle row: Mr Gill, Mr Conway-Jones, Revd Murray-Browne, Mr Hannam-Clarke (senior) and Mr Theo Hannam-Clarke. Front row: Christopher Walker, Stuart Page, Richard Winters, George Poole and Philip Gabb.

The choir at about 1925, in front of the extended north side of the church, in the space now at the side of the church hall. From left to right, back row: Mr G. Long, -?-, Mr R. Morris, Mr W. Gibbs, Mr R. Iles, Mr Judd, -?-, -?-, Mr J. Jeans, -?-. Front row: -?-, James Wilkes, -?-, -?-, -?-, -?-, Mr F. Cope, Revd Jesson, Mr A. Wilkes, Cecil Berry, Geoffrey Cole, -?-, -?-, -?-.

A class from the council school outside the north door of the main school building *c.*1908. The teacher is probably Miss Bordiss.

Another group at the council school, thought to be *c.*1922. The teacher at the left is probably student teacher Miss I. Barnes. The other teacher is probably Mrs Berry, wife of the headmaster.

Miss Page and children at her school c.1927. From left to right, back row: Bobby Spencer, Roma Spencer, Mary Price and Bernard Martin. Centre row: Bobby Raynes, Miss Page and Harold Norton. Front row: Peggy Townsend, Peggy Fowles, David Spencer, Mary Page and Janet English.

Children of Miss Page's school, c.1930. From left to right, back row: Bobby Raynes, Mary Page, Peggy Fowles, Janet English and Cecil Pope. Centre row: Oscar Colburn, Sheila Henley, Joyce Bicknell, Yvonne Jones, Prudence Cole and John Foster. Front row: Ronald Colburn, Joyce Colwell, Jean Colburn, Nancy Buckingham, Jean Fowles and Raymond Tincknell.

The final group of children at Miss Page's school. This is probably c.1946, and the school ceased shortly after this.

A group photograph, probably of the whole of the council school in the church hall c.1933. Mr Wakefield, the head teacher at the rear, also Mrs Matthews and the scarcely visible Miss Belcher.

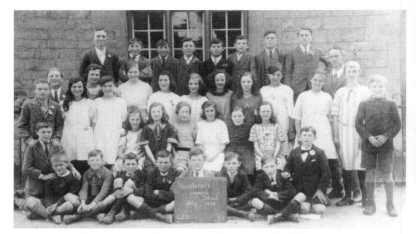

A council school group in 1924. From left to right back row: Fred Hawker, Ted Chandler, Leslie Stubbs, Robert Hopton, Arthur Mustoe, William Howells, Frank Cooper, Ernest Berry and Mr E. Pearson. Third row: Harold Miles, John Busson, Ethel Medcroft, Ruby Hartwell, Molly Bircher, Gladys Neale, Violet Wood, Alice Rudge, Margery Goode, Phyllis Betteridge, Doris Wood, Nora Hopkins, Rose Restall and Leslie Rudge. Second Row: Robert Smith, Linda Pratt, Kitty Bircher, Kathleen Mann, Edith Bircher, Matilda Miles, Nora Elborough and John Long. Front row: Fred Tunley, Jack Bircher, Joseph Close, Edward Close, John Hayward, Stanley Wilson and Leslie Cole.

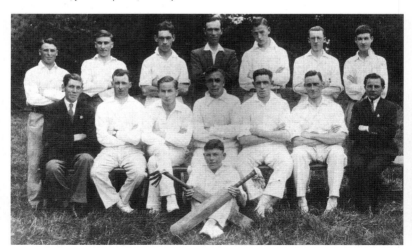

Hucclecote Cricket Club, a photograph of 1927 in a field near Old Green Farm.

A further council school group in July 1924. Presumably taken on the same day as the picture opposite. From left to right, back row: Anthony Wood, Albert Bevan, Lionel Hawker, George Wood, Leslie Cole, Henry Tyndall, James Barry and Frank Barry. Third row: Doreen Twyning, Bessie Reeves, Brenda Carliss, Emily Bevan, Mildred Long, Freda Howells, Blanche Wallace, Ada Busson, Maud Elton and Mrs Matthews. Second Row: Rose Miles, -?- Gardner, Joyce Warren, Clarice Hartwell, Ethel Close, Kitty Hawkins, Dolly Long, Mary Chandler, Connie Bircher, Evelyn Hayward and Mary Tunley. Front row: James Thomas, Harold Lindsay, Thomas Rudge, Donald Long, Ernest Philpotts, William Middleton and Basil Wallace.

Hucclecote Cricket Club, an informal picture c.1939.

Hucclecote Rugby Football Club, *c.*1919. The photograph appears to have been taken in the school playground to the north of the building.

Ladies sewing group, on the back lawn of Hucclecote House, *c.*1882.

A group of local lads outside the 'Ark', c.1931. They had built this themselves and lived in it for a lark. It stood near the bridleway leading to the far end of Green Lane. From left to right, back row: Bill Bircher, Ernest Berry and Bert Hopton. Front row: Leslie Cole, Fred Tunley, Edgar Tunley and Bob Hopton.

A similar group to above with some instruments, some of which they may have made themselves.

A loaded tram at the terminus bringing trippers to see Sydney Pickles and his flying machine.

SYDNEY PICKLES
AT. HUCCLECOTE. MAR 1913

Sydney Pickles with his monoplane in the field opposite the Top Shop.

The Hucclecote floods of 19 May 1924, when the brook overflowed and much damage was done. Water running down the main road outside the 'Top Shop'.

The 1924 floods at Dinglewell, the view to Foxall Road. The course of the brook can be seen by the line of turbulence, with some damage near the bridge on the left.

The Hucclecote Local Defence Volunteers, later named the Home Guard.
This photograph is c.1940 and possibly includes some men from other parishes.

The prizewinners at the annual show, 1947. A wonderful photographic composition and my
favourite photograph in the book. A happy scene and an evocative glimpse of life during the
post-war years.

The funeral procession for the several victims of the German bomb that destroyed a number of houses near the Royal Oak in 1942.

Clearing away the bomb damage in 1942. This view is to the west of the Royal Oak, looking towards Brockworth.

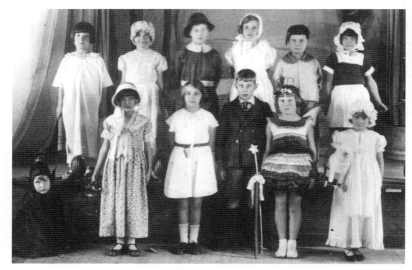

A council school group from 'Land of Nursery Rhyme'; an item in the concert in the church hall, 1932. From left to right, back row: Geraldine Maxfield, Edna Maxfield, Robert Roberts, Vera Banks, Eddie Parsloe and Diana Brewer. Front row: Fred Workman, Margaret Done, Joyce Hearn, Peter Cooper, Betty Hayward and Sylvia Medcroft.

The horse-drawn Church Army Mission Van outside Hucclecote Church in 1905, during a tour of parishes which had followed its consecration at College Green, Gloucester.

Five

Gloster Aircraft Company

A view of the airfield, with the Malvern Hills as a backdrop, *c.* 1930. The airfield originated as an Air Board acceptance park during the First World War.

A low-level view of the aerodrome buildings in 1929. In the foreground is the Fairmile area with the pond from the old brickworks.

From previous page: A low level aerial view of the aerodrome buildings, with Hucclecote fields in the background, 1929. The Gloster Aircraft Company had only moved in to the complete site in the previous year, when they finally left their Cheltenham base and bought the airfield and buildings from the Government.

GREBE (SERVICE TYPE)

The Grebe was a radial-engined fighter supplied in quantity to the RAF in 1924. It had a top speed of 151 mph from its 395 hp Bristol Aeroplane Jupiter IV engine. The Grebe was used in trials in 1926 for assessing the possibilities of launching fighters from airships.

An unidentified photograph of a Gloster fighter at Hucclecote, with houses on Ermin Street clearly to be seen in the background. This is probably the Gamecock, successor to the Grebe and an immensely popular GAC design in the later 1920s. Like the Grebe and other predecessors, this aeroplane was of all-wood construction.

The Gorcock single seater fighter. This aeroplane was based upon the Gamecock but was the first Gloster aircraft to use an all-metal airframe. With a 550 hp direct-drive Napier Lion VIII engine the Gorcock attained a speed of 174 mph at 5,000 feet.

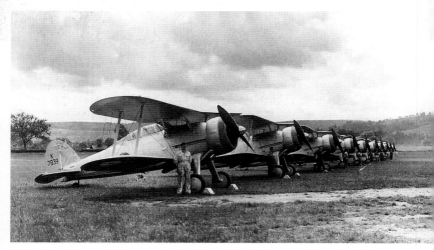

A line of ten Gloster Gladiators ready for delivery. The RAF acquired their first Gladiators in February 1937 and at the time of the Munich crisis in September 1938 had six squadrons of Gladiators together with nine squadrons of Gauntlets, the Gladiator's predecessor.

Hawker Typhoons being assembled at Hucclecote during the Second World War.

Ten months before the last Hurricane left the Hucclecote factory, its successor, the Typhoon, was appearing on the production lines. The Hurricane had been built at Hawker Aircraft, the Austin Motor Company and at Gloster Aircraft Company. The production of the Typhoon was unique to Glosters and in total 3,330 aeroplanes were built between 1941 and 1945.

Page 112 bottom: W4041/G, the first Gloster E.28/39 (Whittle Jet) at Hucclecote, May 1941. It first made short hops at Hucclecote, 8 May 1941. It was then taken by road to Lincolnshire, and the first proper flight was made from RAF Cranwell on 15 May 1941. The Lincolnshire site was chosen for secrecy as Hucclecote was overlooked from hills and in a relatively high population area.

This prototype served as an experimental frame for a number of different jet engines, with power being increased successively from engine to engine as new developments were made. The first engine, the Whittle design, Power Jets W.1 engine developed 860 lb thrust. By the end of 1943 the experimentation enabled Power Jets to produce an engine (W.2/500) capable of producing 1,760 lb thrust.

This aeroplane was donated to the Science Museum in 1946, a fitting tribute to pioneering work in jet aviation.

Hawker Typhoons being assembled at Hucclecote.

The Gloster E.28/39 at Hucclecote, May 1941.

The Gloster Meteor. The world's first production jet fighter entered service with the RAF in 1944 and was used initially in the fight against the V1 rockets. They were able to fly fast enough to catch the V1's and 'tip' the fins of the rocket throwing the gyroscope off-balance.

Gloster Gladiator K8032 being prepared by Gloster apprentices in readiness for presentation to the Shuttleworth Trust, November 1960.

The last Gloster success, the Javelin, was built between 1955 and 1960. It entered service with the RAF in January 1956.

The Javelin was built as an all-weather fighter. Experience in Korea had highlighted the need for a bomber-support aircraft capable of destroying interceptors over enemy bases and its bombers early in their outward flight. It had two crew with armament of guns, rocket batteries and guided weapons. The aircraft's performance was high-subsonic.

Six

Brockworth

The main road at Brockworth just past the old GAC factory, looking towards the Cross Hands, with the lane to the golf club on the right, c.1933. The land on the right just past Golf Club Lane was used for the 1938 aeroplane factory which later became British Nylon Spinners, later ICI Fibres, and now Du Pont.

The main road at Brockworth, almost opposite what was later to become the Ermin Park junction, looking east, c.1925.

From previous page: A peacock topiary embellishing a house at Brockworth, c.1890.

116

Green Street, c.1914.

Green Street, a similar view to the picture above, but some twenty years or more later. This picture thought to be c.1938, shortly after the houses were built.

Guise Cottage and old post office *c.*1930. Unfortunately this fine timbered cottage was burned down in September 1976. This view is taken looking across Ermin Street with the large telegraph poles clearly visible.

Guise Cottage, a view from the north side. It stood on the corner where Vicarage Lane met Ermin Street.

Green Street, with a clear view of Cooper's Hill, *c.*1939.

Butts Pitch, Brockworth, *c.*1920. This photograph shows the dramatic change that Brockworth has undergone over the past seventy years. The semi-rural street scene with early-nineteenth-century brick and stone cottages has been replaced by suburban development. The name 'Butts' come from the days of medieval archery practice when it was mandatory for all able bodied men of the parish to practice archery.

Above: The Cross Hands Inn, 1922. This view is taken looking across Ermin Street towards Shurdington. Note the narrow roads and the lack of telegraph poles. However, road traffic had built up sufficiently to justify the R.A.C. box on the right of the picture.

Below: A clear picture of the old Cross Hands photographed *c.*1930. The inn was demolished in 1937.

Above and below: Two more views of the old Cross Hands Inn, possibly taken for R.A.C. promotional purposes, *c.*1936. The top picture has been taken looking towards Witcombe, the bottom picture looking towards Cheltenham. Notice how the R.A.C. motorbike has been moved to remain in view, while the patrolman casually chats to the policeman on point duty.

The newly-built Cross Hands Inn and the brand new roundabout photographed in 1939 shortly before the outbreak of war. Note that the original roundabout was considerably larger than the present structure. These were a novelty in the 1930s and demonstrate how the traffic problem was perceived that required police point duty at these crossroads even with the minimal traffic level when compared to the 1990s problems.

Robinson Hall photographed shortly before its collapse and final demolition in 1982. It was built in 1929 in a mock-tudor style as a village hall for Brockworth.

Seven

Brockworth
People and Events

All of the children of Brockworth National School in 1935. Photographed in the field adjacent to the school on the A46 with the bank as a backdrop. The head teacher was Miss D. Hutt.

The total complement of the same school in July 1952, this time viewed from the bank in the field looking across the Severn Vale. The falling attendance role led to the closure of the school in 1960.

The erection of the may pole for the cheese rolling of 1924. The master of ceremonies in this year as in many previous years was William Brookes, pictured here standing behind a small boy to the left of the may pole.

The funeral procession of William Brookes in 1933. William was M.C. for the cheese rolling events for over fifty years and presented himself in a white smock together with a decorated top hat. He carried a small stick which he raised to start off every cheese race down the hill.

Tea in the garden at Windyridge Cottage, Cooper's Hill. This photograph of 1923 shows Mrs Gregory, Ellen Lander, Roy Mitchell and Mrs Mitchell.

The start of the procession in Mill Lane for the first Brockworth Carnival, May 1970, in which Frankie Vaughan made a guest appearance and opened the carnival.

Brockworth Congregational Church sunday school outing, 1960. The Revd Tal James is pictured on the right-hand side.

The opening ceremony of the dual-purpose church hall, March 1957. This hall served as church as well as a hall until the new congregational church was built in 1960.

This fine view from Cooper's Hill provides a tail-piece for the book. It shows the newly-built Cross Hands c.1940 and the fields on the left now covered by housing developments from the 1950s, 1960s and 1970s. Robinson Hall stands in the foreground.

Acknowledgements

My thanks go to all those people who kindly lent photographs or postcards that have been included in this book. The contribution from Mr Anthony Done was invaluable, and without his pioneering work in gathering together photographic material this book would not have been possible. Mrs Rosemary Hellerman was most helpful in supplying pictures for Brockworth and Mr Nigel Brown supplied some wonderful photographs of GAC aircraft, to the point where it is worth considering a separate book on the GAC years alone! Mention should also be made of photographs collected by the Late Mr H. Middleton which provided a useful record for Hucclecote.

In addition I wish to thank Mr Russell Adams; Mr L.E. Copeland; Mrs Rose Hitchings; Mr D. Middleton; Gloucestershire Collection, Gloucester City Library and Gloucestershire Record Office.